Gary Jones

The Best of Lisbon For Short Stay Travel

First published by Gary Jones in 2016.

Copyright © Gary Jones, 2016.

All rights reserved. No part of this publication may be reproduced, stored, or transmitted in any form or by any means, electronic, mechanical, photocopying, recording, scanning, or otherwise without written permission from the publisher. It is illegal to copy this book, post it to a website, or distribute it by any others means without permission.

This book was professionally typeset on Reedsy.
Find out more at reedsy.com

Contents

Lisbon Introduction	5
A Brief History of Lisbon	8
Transport and Safety in Lisbon	13
Areas of Lisbon	21
Best Time To Visit	26
Lisbon's Best Museums	28
The Best Art Galleries in the City	33
Best Coffee Shops in Lisbon	37
Lisbon's Best Bars and Night Clubs	42
Top 5 Affordable Hotels	45
Top 5 Restaurants	49
Special Things You Can ONLY DO in Lisbon	53
3-Day Itinerary	59
Conclusion	61

1

Lisbon Introduction

I want to thank you for downloading my book!!
Here's a quick overview of what this book offers:
-Learn about the city's rich history
-Find out the best way to get around the city

-Learn safety tips when touring Lisbon
-Figure out the different neighborhoods and their unique characteristics
-Understand the best time to visit the city
-Explore the city's rich history through remarkable artifacts in their best museums
-Discover Portuguese art in Lisbon's best galleries
-Find out where the best coffee and pastries are served in Lisbon

-Know where to go for late night party
-Stay on budget with the top 5 affordable Lisbon hotels
-Have a unique gastronomic experience at the Lisbon's top restaurants
-Build memories of a lifetime by trying out something special you can only do in Lisbon

Plus, we give you a head start at planning your trip with our sample 3-day itinerary!

Thanks again for downloading this book, I hope you enjoy it!

2

A Brief History of Lisbon

UMA BREVE HISTÓRIA
A Brief History of Lisbon

Lisbon has survived through the ups and downs from amassing immense riches to suffering plagues, fires, revolutions, earthquakes, coups and dictatorship. Today, Lisbon stands strong as a beautiful city attracting many visitors from the world over, admiring its unique characteristics.

The rich history of the through the ages
From the Ancient Years

Many believe that Ulysses was the first one to land in Lisbon on his way home from the Trojan War. Its ancient name, Ulissipo or Olissipo means "enchanted port." The sure thing is that the Phoenicians settled here around 3,000 years ago. The Phoenicians gave it the name, Alis Ubbo which means "delightful shore." After the Phoenicians, the Greeks, Carthaginians and Romans eventually realized what a delight this place was.

Even then, Lisbon witnessed tribal chaos. The North African Moors emerged victorious. They ruled the land in 714. The Moors called it Lissabona. In an effort to defend the city from the Christians, the

Moors put up fortifications. They continued to defend the city for 400 years.

In 1147 however, Christian fighters led by Dom Alfonso Henriques took over the city. In 1260, Alfonso III chose Lisbon as the capital because of its strategic central location and reliable ports.

When Vasco de Gama discovered a sea route to India, Lisbon became more productive. It rose as an opulent center for a vast empire. The city continued to soar in the 1800s after the discovery of gold in Brazil. Merchants came to Lisbon to trade jewels, silks, spices and gold.

Along with the growth of trade, architecture flourished during this era. It spoke of extravagance. Among the masterpieces built during this period include Manueline works like Belém's Mosteiro dos Jerónimos.

Earthquake Shook Lisbon

Everything was going so well until November 1, 1755 when three devastating earthquakes hit the city. The tremors created destructive tsunami and started fires all over Lisbon. 90,000 souls out of 270,000 were lost. The city was in ruins. There was a big question whether Lisbon will be able to regain it's former glorious status. Marquês de Pombal, the chief minister of Dom João I took charge of rebuilding the city. The goal was to create a simple and easy to manage style which is now very much visible.

Chaos Continued to Plague Lisbon

Just as the city was getting back on its feet, Lisbon fell into a series of chaos. Napoleon and his forces took over the city in November 1807. They held Lisbon hostage for four years.

After Napoleon, the Republican movement grew stronger. In 1908, it became more turbulent when Dom Carlos and his son were assassinated in Lisbon at the Praça do Comércio. For the next 16 years, the city went under 45 changes in government. Lisbon witnessed another major assassination in 1918. President Sidónio Pais was killed at the Rossio station.

Second World War

In the Second World War, Lisbon played a neutral role. However, a great number of spies went to the city.

In 1926 and 1974, coups shook the order in the city. In 1974 and the following year, refugees from the former African colonies flooded the city. It added to Lisbon's cultural diversity.

Lisbon Getting Back on Its Feet

In 1986, Portugal came to join the European Community. It proved to be an excellent move. With the help of funds sent by the European Community, development restarted in the city. It was a much-needed help after fire destroyed Chiado in 1988. Facilities were improved and the streets were cleaned.

Lisbon was back on track. In fact, the city started hosting major events including the 1994 European City of Culture, the 1998 Expo and the 2004 European Football Championships.

In 2006, the city continued to bloom. Many development projects around the city were started and completed. This includes the restoration and reopening of the Praça de Touros or Lisbon's bullring. The metro system was improved, and an Alfama building rehab began construction.

After all the challenges, Lisbon has not lost its delightful charm. Many visitors from around the world flock the city to experience all that this beautiful city has to offer.

3

Transport and Safety in Lisbon

VIAJE COM SEGURANÇA
Getting Into Lisbon
If you are flying into Lisbon, you will arrive at Lisbon Portela Airport.Getting into the city is easy using one of the transport options.Click the Airport link for transport into Lisbon.

Lisbon International Airport Website
http://www.ana.pt/en-US/Aeroportos/lisboa/Lisboa/PlanYour-Trip/Public-Transport/Pages/Public-Transport.aspx

Lisbon International Airport Map
https://goo.gl/maps/XdBzgdSnznm

Transport and Safety in Lisbon

The streets of Lisbon are quite busy, which results to heavy traffic. Unless you are exploring farther districts like the Belém, you are better off wandering about the city center on foot. In case you need wheels to get you where you want to go, you can depend on the following means of transportation around Lisbon.

City Trasport by By CARRIS

This is the operator for Lisbon's trains, subways, funiculars and buses. Tourist tickets can be bought from CARRIS booths, network train stations and Metro stations. A 1-day pass costs 3.70€. Bring your passport as it is a requirement for buying a tourist ticket.

CARRIS Website
http://carris.transporteslisboa.pt/en/home/

By Metro

The large M signs stand for Metro. Single tickets are sold for 0.80€ while a 1 day pass will cost you 3.70€. The Metro is likely to be crowded on bullfight days. A lot of people take the transport to get to Campo Pequeno from Avenida da República. Transport is open from 6:30am to 1am.

An interesting thing about Lisbon Metro is the impressive art collection on display. When you get the chance to take the transport, do not miss lineup of sculptures, glazed tiles and paintings. You will see here some of the contemporary art work of famous and renowned

Portuguese artists like Maria Helena Vieira da Silva and Maria Keil. You'll get to see fine art works on display at the following Metro stations: Marquês de Pombal, Campo Grande, Baixa/Chiado and Cais do Sodré.

By Bus or Tram

These are the cheapest forms of public transport in the city. The steep way up to the Bairro Alto can be accessed through the eléctricos or trams. Lisbon also has double-decker buses as seen in the streets of London. Basic fare is at 1.40€. These public transportations run from 6am to 1am.

If the Metro has an impressive fine art collection, there are also antediluvian eléctricos which resemble the cable cars of San Francisco. They are no longer just a means of transport. The antediluvian eléctricos have become quite famous as a tourist attraction too.

Bus or Tram Website

http://carris.transporteslisboa.pt/en/home/

By Train

If you want to go from Lisbon to another village or town, it is best to take the electric train. It has a single class of seat. The tickets are affordable and generally comfortable. From Lisbon, hop in from the waterfront Cais do Sodré Station. 1 way ticket costs 1.80€ to 4€ depending on where you are heading.

Cais do Sodré Station Map

https://goo.gl/maps/nG8tMvPuhKJ2

By Funiculars

There are three funiculars in Lisbon: the Glória, the Bica and the Lavra. Glória runs from Praça dos Restauradores to Rua São Pedro de Alcântara. Bica takes the Calçada do Combro to Rua da Boavista route. Lavra can take you from east of Avenida da Liberdade to the Campo Mártires da Pátria. A one-way ticket costs 1.40€.

By Ferry
Taking the ferry is wise if you want to avoid the heavy traffic. You

will also be treated with a scenic view. If you're heading to Cacilhas, take the boat from either Praça do Comércio or Cais do Sodré. You will be dropped off at the Estação do Barreiro from which you can take a train to head to Algarve or Costa Azul.

Ferries run throughout the day every 15 to 20 minutes. Travel time is around 15 minutes. A trip from Lisbon to Cacilhas costs 0.81€.

Praça do Comércio Map
https://goo.gl/maps/2JPGv45Tnyy
Cais do Sodré Map
https://goo.gl/maps/TtdyoCtR9nE2

By Taxi

As compared to other major cities, Lisbon taxi fare is not as expensive which makes it a popular means of transportation in the city. The basic fare starts at 2.50€ which will take you as far as 153m. An additional 0.10€ is added to the basic fare for every 162m travelled. There will be a 20 percent additional if you're taking the taxi between 10pm and 6am. If you're carrying luggage that weighs over 66 pounds, the driver is allowed to charge you additional 50 percent. The standard tip is 20 percent.

By Car

Lisbon is congested. That said, it is not wise to rent and drive a car if you're going around the city. Car rentals are only advisable if you're taking a trip out of town.

Is Lisbon Safe for Tourists?

Lisbon is generally safe for tourists but just like other major cities, pickpockets and petty crimes are unavoidable. Be careful, especially around crowded areas like train and tram stations. Take usual precautions like wearing money belt to protect your belongings. You have to watch out for hash sellers too. Best of all, you should use your common sense. Don't do anything that you would not think about doing at home, in your own city.

Bring a good city map with you and familiarize yourself with the neighborhoods so you have lesser chances of getting lost. It's good to learn a few Portuguese words. If you can't then don't worry about it. You are likely to find locals who speak English willing to lend a helping hand.

Obtain visitor information from the tourist office located at the Palácio da Foz. The office is open from 9am to 8pm. You can also buy a Lisbon card here so you can avail of free city transportation. The Lisbon card also includes admission to museums and other city attractions. It can also be used to avail of discounts to events.
Palácio da Foz Map
https://goo.gl/maps/sJK18GvuZrF2

The Lisbon 1-day pass for adults costs 16€, 27€ for a 2-day pass and 34€ for a 3-day pass. Children between 5 and 11 years old can get a 1-day pass for 9.50€, 14€ for 2-day pass and 17€ for 3-day pass.

You can contact the main tourist office at phone number, 21/12-05-050.

4

Areas of Lisbon

VAMOS PARA LISBOA
Areas of Lisbon

Here are the major areas in Lisbon and must-see places in each neighborhood.

Baixa

Lisbon's business district boasts of its buildings structured according to the Pombaline-style architecture, the simplistic and easy to manage style after the earthquake destroyed the city. The area houses Portuguese banks. The area includes the clothing stores at Rua Augusta. This is where you will find the goldsmiths and silversmiths at Rua

Áurea and Rua da Prata respectively.
Baixa Map
https://goo.gl/maps/PqqucK5wWDB2

Chiado

The west of Baixa leads to this neighborhood known as Lisbon's shopping district. The finest shops in Lisbon like the famous porcelain and china store, Vista Alegre is found here. A Brasileira, the coffee shop where Portuguese literati gather is also located in this area.
Chiado Map
https://goo.gl/maps/vRC7aoimoxm

Bairro Alto

If you continue the climb from Chiado, you will reach Bairro Alto which means "Upper City." It is best to get to this area through a trolley car. Many of the buildings here were untouched by the destructive that hit the city in 1755. Among the things you will find in this neighborhood are excellent restaurants, exciting bars and nightclubs as well as charming antique shops. You have to be careful threading the streets at night though, as addicts and drug dealers hang out here.
Bairro Alto Map
https://goo.gl/maps/sBKQeyitnEU2

The Alfama

This is Lisbon's oldest district. It is also known as the Moorish section. Most of the structures here were saved from the earthquake. This neighborhood is home to fishwives or varinas, fishermen and stevedores.

Also found in this area is the Visigothic fortification which the Romans used which is known as the Castelo São Jorge or St. George's Castle. As you climb up Alfama, you will pass by a major landmark, the House of the Pointed Stones or Casa dos Bicos. It is a 16th century townhouse with diamond-shaped stones adorning its facade. Avoid wandering in this neighborhood at night. Some parts of Alfama are where muggers wait for unsuspecting victims.

The Alfama Map
https://goo.gl/maps/QD2Pyzyf2U32

Belém

The suburban part of the city, Belém houses the Portugal's fine monuments that were built in the Age of Discovery. Before the 1755 earthquake, Belém used to be an aristocratic sector where elegant town houses abound.

Tourists flock the area for two reasons: Mosteiro dos Jerónimos and the Museu Nacional dos Coches. Mosteiro dos Jerónimos is a Manueline structure built in the 16th century. The Museu Nacional dos Coches or National Coach Museum is unique and considered the finest the world has ever seen. Regarded as the land of museums in the city, Belém also houses the Museu de Marinha and the Museu de Arte Popular.

Belém Map
https://goo.gl/maps/Gu1YdY3jhLM2

Cacilhas

The neighborhood of the working class, Cacilhas also houses the best seafood restaurants in the city. It can be accessed through a ferry ride from the Praça do Comércio or through the Ponte do 25 de Abril. Constructed in 1966, this bridge stretches 2.2km long and towers at 190m height. Ponte do 25 de Abril has the longest suspension is all the bridges in Europe. Another notable structure in this neighborhood is the Ponte Vasco da Gama that makes the north of Portugal, southern Algarve, east of Alentejo and southern Spain more accessible.

Cacilhas Map
https://goo.gl/maps/YZZiHxQDTZx

Uptown

Uptown Lisbon is both a residential and business district consisting of 20th century apartments and office buildings. It houses the Calouste

Gulbenkian Museum, the Fronteira Palace and the Campo Pequeno. This is also where one of Europe's largest shopping malls is found, the Colombo along with the post-modern Amoreiras.

Uptown Map
https://goo.gl/maps/gkHDTXdT7Ak

5

Best Time To Visit

Lisbon has a nice location, seated in southeast Europe. This means the city enjoys hot summers with cool wind coming from the Atlantic. The winters are mild here too. The average temperature in July and August is at 79.3°F. The temperate winter averages at 60°F. Rain, however, falls heavily between November and March. That means Lisbon is good to visit for most parts of the year. The city does not run out of reasons to celebrate throughout the year with an impressive list of events.

The city of Lisbon greets the year with a series of festivals. The list includes Lisbon Fish & Flavours. The gastronomic festival is a delight for foodies. Classes and demonstrations are also held in the Commerce Square during the event.

By April, Lisbon holds a Book Fair at the Edward VII Park where colorful stalls are set up. But the biggest event of the year by far is the Festas de Lisboa of June where the streets of the city center and the Alfama are greeted by a barrage of music, parties, parades and dances.

In August, the city prepares for the Jazz em Agosto. The event pays tribute to jazz music. Live bands play at the Calouste Gulbenkian Foundation. In November, Arte de Lisbon is held at the Nation's Park. By year end, Lisbon holds a series of New Year's Eve concerts and exciting firework displays at the Commerce Square.

Now you can schedule your trip according to the event you'd like to see in Lisbon.

6

Lisbon's Best Museums

VAMOS EXPLORAR A HISTÓRIA
Lisbon's Best Museums
One of the top reasons why visitors from all over the world come to Lisbon is the exquisite line-up of museums. Lisbon's rich history is depicted in various art forms. If you want to learn more about Lisbon's

amazing story, you better check out at least one of these museums.

Calouste Gulbenkian Museum

This great museum in Lisbon carries one of the finest art collections in all of Europe. On display are more than 6,000 art pieces that were accumulated for more than 4,000 years. Some of these paintings date back to antiquity. These art pieces were once owned by Calouste Gulbekian, an Armenian oil magnate, who donated his estate to the nation. The museum dedicated to this man was inaugurated in 1960.

You should allot at least 2 hours to go through these valuable artifacts. Among the must-sees are the Roman medallions which were found in Egypt, Thomas Germain's crafted silverware, Turner's The Wreck of a Transport Ship, Armenian illustrated manuscripts from the 16th century and the Noveau jewelry by Lalique.

To get to this museum, take the Metro to either São Sebastião or Praça de Espanha Stations.
Address: Avenida de Berna, 45A, Uptown Lisbon
Phone: +351 217 823 000
Opening Hours: Wed-Mon, 10am-6pm
Calouste Gulbenkian Museum Website
http://gulbenkian.pt/museu/Museu/en/Homepage
Calouste Gulbenkian Museum Map
https://goo.gl/maps/ZoDfVp3v94U2

Museu do Oriente

Portugal has forged cultural links with the Orient. The artifacts displayed in this museum are proof of that. The highlights include the 17th-century Namban screen which depicts the arrival of Portuguese explorers in Japan and the intricate teak door from India. This door is said to date back to the 18th century. It has beautiful bronze and iron trimmings too. Another special feature of the museum is an exceptional piece from Macau. It is a child's cradle in the shape of a boat. There are also exquisite silver alloy bracelets from East Timor.

Address: Doca de Alcantara, Lisbon, 1350-352

Phone: +351 21 358 5200

Opening Hours: Fri (10am-10pm), Tue-Thu, Sat-Sun (10am-8pm)

Museu do Oriente Website

http://www.museudooriente.pt/?lang=en

Museu do Oriente Map

https://goo.gl/maps/39hh35xvg6z

Museu Nacional do Azulejo

This museum is dedicated to decorative tiles or what the Portuguese call, azulejo. Located in the historical Convento da Madre de Deus from 1509, Museu Nacional do Azulejo's tiles are displayed in a chronological order.

The exhibit starts with the early 16th century Moorish tiles with multi-colored design. One of the highlights is the Nossa Senhora daVida altar piece which showcases the development of Portugal's own style of tile making. There's another interesting piece, a 35-metre tiled panorama representing Lisbon before it was ruined by the 1755 earthquake. It is known as Portugal's longest azulejo. Admission to the museum includes entry to the Madre de Deus church.

Address: Rua da Madre de Deus,4 Lisbon, 1900-312

Phone: +351 21 810 0340

Opening Hours: Tue-Sun (10am-6pm)

Museu Nacional do Azulejo Website

http://www.museudoazulejo.pt/en-GB/default.aspx

Museu Nacional do Azulejo Map

https://goo.gl/maps/TavXXASzNHC2

Museu Escola de Artes Decorativas da Fundação Ricardo do Espírito Santo

Located in the Palácio Azurara, the museum has an impressive collection of paintings, textiles, ceramics, pieces of furniture, gold and silver from the 17th and 18th centuries. Do not miss the exquisite ornate rooms. The biggest highlight includes the 1510 tapestry woven in silk and wool, the ewer with King Manuel I's armillary sphere from the Ming Dynasty and the 18th century woolen carpet which comes from Arraiolos.

Address: Largo das Portas do Sol 2 Lisbon, 1100-564
Phone: +351 21 881 4600
Opening Hours: Wed-Mon (10am-5pm)
Museu Escola de Artes Website
http://www.fress.pt/
Museu Escola de Artes Map
https://goo.gl/maps/Y4UaPBbhtTU2

MUDE — Museu do Design e da Moda

This interesting museum is located in what used to be a bank. Museu Design Moda has some of the most interesting designs and fashion classics. The exhibit focuses on vintage apparel. The works of haute couture designers from the 50s and 60s like Yves Saint Laurent and Coco Chanel are on display here. There are designs from Giorgio Armani, Paco Rabanne, Vivien Westwood and Mary Quant as well.

Interior designers like Ray Eames, Charles and Phillipe Starck are also well represented in the museum. There are a few surprises for visitors like a Piaggo classic Italian scooter. Everything in this museum is a fashion delight.

Address: Rua Augusta 24, Lisbon, 1100-053
Phone: +351 21 888 6117
Opening Hours: Tue-Sun (10am-6pm)
MUDE Website
http://www.mude.pt/?lang=en
MUDE Map

https://goo.gl/maps/kpTWqMtS9k82

Museu de Marinha

Found in the Jerónimos monastery, this is one of the most engaging museums in Lisbon. The focus of the museum is maritime history and is dedicated to Portugal's seafaring tradition. The tour starts at the Discoveries Hall displaying intricate model ships. These displays showcase the development of ship building starting from the 15th century onwards.

Museu de Marinha also has a vast collection of astrolabe which is the biggest in the world. It includes a Willem Jansz Blaeu's terrestrial globe from 1645. You should watch out for the royal yacht of Amélia and its exquisite wood panel cabin constructed in 1900. There are plenty of maritime paraphernalia on display too like navigational instruments and charts. In the main building, you will find the Santa Cruz which is a seaplane used to cross the trans-south Atlantic in 1922.

Address: Praça do Império, Lisbon, 1400-206
Phone: +351 21 362 0019
Opening Hours: Daily (9am-5pm)
Museu de Marinha Website
http://museu.marinha.pt/pt/Paginas/default.aspx
Museu de Marinha Map
https://goo.gl/maps/BAatD2kHJaN2

7

The Best Art Galleries in the City

The Best Art Galleries in the City

Because of Portugal's rich culture and history, artists can draw inspiration from many things. Lisbon prides itself as a patron of the arts. Many galleries have been established to support artists of the past and the present. If you like art and curious to see what Portuguese artists come up with, do drop by at least one of these amazing galleries.

Museu Nacional de Arte Antiga

This is the country's national gallery. Its vast collection of Portuguese paintings from the 15th and 16th centuries is the largest in Portugal. It also features stunning European paintings from the middle ages up to the 19th century. In addition to paintings, Museu Nacional de Arte Antiga also has an extensive display of applied art; most of which are from the Discover age and Exploration era.

A 17th century palace houses the museum. The highlights include the Nuno Gonçalves' exquisite Panels of St Vincent from 1470 and Hieronymus Bosch's The Temptations of St Anthony.

Address: Rua das Janelas Verdes 9, Lisbon, 1249-017
Phone: +351 21 391 2800
Opening Hours: Wed-Sun (10am-6pm), Tue (2pm-6pm)
Museu Nacional de Arte Antiga Website
http://www.museudearteantiga.pt/english
Museu Nacional de Arte Antiga Map
https://goo.gl/maps/XjquQojUaBq

Alecrim 50 Galeria de Arte

A newly opened art gallery, Alecrim 50 Galeria de Arte was established in 2006 and is located in Chiado. The main goal of the gallery is to promote the works of artists while they are still in their career's early stages. They put on display art works that demonstrate innovation, unquestionable talent and superior creativity. The art works on display vary from paintings to photography, sculptures to installation art.

Address: 50 Rua Alecrim, Lisbon, Portugal
Phone: +351 21 346 5258
Opening Hours: Tue-Sat (2pm-7pm)
Alecrim 50 Galeria de Arte Website
http://www.alecrim50.pt/
Alecrim 50 Galeria de Arte Map

https://goo.gl/maps/mgnYEuJeyXP2

Centro de Arte Moderna

Established in 1983, this art gallery showcases art collection from the 20th to 21st century. Centro de Arte Moderna also sets up temporary exhibits featuring the works of homegrown talents and international artists. Its permanent collection consists of 9,000 pieces focused on Portuguese art. Among those on display are the works of Antonio Dacosta, a Portuguese painter that spearheaded the surrealist movement in the country. There are magnificent works from Amadeo de Souza Cardoso as well, the forefather of modernism in Portugal. Drawings, paintings and objects from the Portuguese visual storyteller, Paula Rego.

Address: Rua Dr Nicolau de Bettencourt, Lisbon
Phone: +351 21 782 3474
Opening Hours: Wed-Mon (10am-6pm)
Centro de Arte Moderna Website
http://gulbenkian.pt/cam/
Centro de Arte Moderna Map
https://goo.gl/maps/kuYD7DaNVLS2

São Mamede Galeria de Arte

Established in the 60s, this art gallery promotes the works of Portuguese contemporary artists. The highlights include the Alexandre Manuel's incomparable black and white photography, António Areal's surrealist sketches and paintings along with Rui Matos' modern sculptures. While it dedicates itself to Portuguese art, São Mamede Galeria de Arte also holds exhibit for international artists like the works of Shintaro Nakaoka, a renowned Japanese sculptor.

Address: 167 Rua da Escola Politénica, Lisbon
Phone: +351 21 397 3255
Opening Hours: Mon-Fri (11am-8pm), Sat (11am-7pm)
São Mamede Galeria de Arte Website

http://www.saomamede.com/
São Mamede Galeria de Arte Map
https://goo.gl/maps/QH0a5pq9j1T2

8

Best Coffee Shops in Lisbon

AMO CAFÉ

Best Coffee Shops in Lisbon

Did you know that the Portuguese spend most of their money and time hanging out in cafés? They surely love to drink coffee and eat some pastries. Coffee shops are an institution in Lisbon. They do not only serve excellent coffee. They also provide an enticing atmosphere with some of the most picturesque views.

If you want coffee, ask for bica or espresso. In this city, strong bica is always paired with a light meal. Aside from their coffee though, you should also try their milky galão or latte and pasteis de nata or custard tarts.

Cruzes Credo Café
After a long walk in Alfama, there's no better way to rest than a seat in a lovely cafe with good customer service and nice music. This is exactly what you get from Cruzes Credo Café. It's a favorite among locals because of their excellent coffee and mouthwatering food.

Do try their burgers and toasts along with their irresistible chocolate cake and gourmet toasts. Their burgers are best enjoyed with natural juice or beer, while the coffee and chocolate cake is a match made in heaven.
Address: Cruzes da Sé, 29, 1100 Lisboa
Phone:+351 21 882 2296
Opening Hours: Daily, 10am-2pm
Cruzes Credo Café Website
https://www.facebook.com/cruzescredo/
Cruzes Credo Café Map
https://goo.gl/maps/MRUy9rUVmoo

Cafe Versailles
If you're heading uptown, you might as well stop by at Cafe Versailles, turn-of-the-century Lisbon café that serves coffee, hot chocolate and sweet pastry. The interior is designed Baroque style adorned with stained glass, engraved mirrors, carved wooden panels and crystal chandeliers. The grand space is quite inviting. Unlike other cafés in the city, the place is less crowded by tourists but locals love it even if

they have to take the metro to get here. Why? Locals say Cafe Versailles has the best pastries in all of Lisbon.

Address: Avenida da Republica, 15a, Uptown Lisbon
Phone: 21 354 6340
Opening Hours: Daily (7:30am-10:00pm)
Cafe Versailles
https://www.facebook.com/Pastelaria-Versailles-125661190814840/
Cafe Versailles
https://goo.gl/maps/PApW41brZ1P2

Café Nicola

This is one of the most popular cafés in Lisbon not just because of its excellent location overlooking the Rossio square. Café Nicola has plenty to offer. For one, it is a historical café where the literary artists from the late 19th century would meet up. The lovely interior is furnished with Art Deco and polished marble adorned with outstanding canvases inspired by Manuel Barbosa du Bocage, a Portuguese poet from the 18th century. Its European café society atmosphere is quite the scene.

The café also has an excellent outdoor terrace where guests can enjoy a spectacular view while sipping their fantastic coffee. The coffee is nothing less than perfection, imported from the world's premier coffee producers, Sao Tome e Principe in South Africa and Brazil. Aside from their great tasting coffee, Café Nicola also serves delicious breakfast.

Address: Praça Dom Pedro IV 24-26 Lisbon
Phone: +351 21 346 0579
Opening Hours: Mon-Fri (8am-10pm) Sat (9am-10pm) Sun (10am-7pm)
Café Nicola Website
https://www.facebook.com/pages/Cafe-Nicola/845684358796213
Café Nicola Map
https://goo.gl/maps/XSUdtJYiSPz

A Brasileira

Lisboans like to meet up at this café before they go to the theatre or see a performance. A Brasileira is more than a hundred years old. The greatest Portuguese poet, Fernando Pessoa, used to hang out here. Journalists, artists and writers back in the day also liked to meet here. When you see this place, you'll be charmed by its lovely interior with the old carved wood and metal décor furnishings. Find a seat outside in the charming terrace and listen to the songs of musicians as they pass by the streets of Chiado.

Address: Rua Garret, 120-122 Lisbon
Phone: +351 213 469 541
Opening Hours: Mon-Sun (8am-2pm)
A Brasileira Website
https://www.facebook.com/pages/Caf%C3%A9-A-Brasileira/114966645183069
A Brasileira Map
https://goo.gl/maps/ijDzsaYdvvw

Café Pastelaria Benard

This is another charming coffee shop but often ignored because it's close to Café A Brasileira. If you are looking for an authentic experience however, without having to squeeze into a crowd, Bernard is the right place to be. It exudes a genuine 19th century atmosphere. Its pastries and cakes are absolutely delicious. The coffee is excellent as well. But Bernard is most known for their chocolate croissants. The lovely terrace is quickly filled up especially in the warm summer months. The locals love coming here for some afternoon tea and yummy sandwiches.

Address: Rua Garrett 104, Lisbon, 1200-205
Phone: +351 21 347 3133
Opening Hours: Daily (8am-11:30pm)
Café Pastelaria Benard Website

https://www.facebook.com/Pastelaria-Benard-342234722482773/
Café Pastelaria Benard Map
https://goo.gl/maps/jthG7pa2FTB2

9

Lisbon's Best Bars and Night Clubs

A NOITE É UMA CRIANÇA
Lisbon's Best Bars and Night Clubs
If you want to chill after a long day of serious touring, you can do so in a cozy bar. Lisbon has plenty to offer. The city has an exciting nightlife and you are more than welcome to join the party!

Clube da Esquina
Located in Bairro Alto, it's a favorite hangout spot not only because it is incredibly inexpensive but also because they serve the most interesting mixes, popular all over the city. Their concoctions include mojitos and caipirinhas but they are most famous for the morangoska.

The atmosphere is mellow and relaxed. It is the perfect place to chill along with the mixed crowd. The DJ plays jazzy-funk soundtracks but the bar also invites guest DJs.
Address: Rua Barroca 30-32, Lisbon
Opening Hours: Daily (7pm-3am)
Clube da Esquina Website
https://www.facebook.com/clubedaesquina.bairroalto
Clube da Esquina Map
https://goo.gl/maps/3AVapDW8dju

Portas Largas

You will have no trouble finding this bar because everybody knows it. Portas Largas or "Large Doors" used to be a fado house. Although it has been transformed into a hip bar, its origin is still apparent. The azulejo panel was maintained along with the old furniture. The ad hoc appeal actually works.

Portas Largas is especially popular in the summer. After ordering a mojito or caipirinha, head outside to Rua da Atalaia and join the laid back crowd. The bar treats its guests with live music from Brazilian or African combo.

Address: Rua da Atalaia 105, Lisbon 1200-038
Opening Hours: Daily 8pm-4am
Portas Largas Website
https://www.facebook.com/pages/Bar-Portas-Largas/181378298544382
Portas Largas Map
https://goo.gl/maps/MuYmtgSxv1o

Station

How cool is it to hang out in a club overlooking the river? You can do that in this funky waterfront Station. The coolest part about this nightclub is the superb sound system. They play a mix of disco-tech and soul. If you want to get inside the club, you have to make a little effort in dressing up. The crowd is fashionable and sophisticated yet the vibe is familiar. Station is especially popular within the glitzy social circuit of Lisbon.

Address: Cais do Gás, Armazém A, Lisbon 1200-109
Opening Hours: Thu-Sat 11pm-6am
Station Website
https://www.facebook.com/stationfoodmusic/
Station Map
https://goo.gl/maps/jV91AhGMjZC2

Cinco Lounge

Sophisticated and cool at the same time. That's the best way to describe Cinco Lounge, a bar run by people who manage Michelin-starred restaurants so you can trust that they know what they are doing. Everything is topnotch from the decor to the service.

It's a little pricey but it comes highly recommended. Try out their freshly original cocktail mixes. And don't miss out on the sushi and other good snacks.
Address: Rua Ruben A. Leitão, 17-A, Principe Real, Lisbon
Website: cincolounge.com
Cinco Lounge Website
https://www.facebook.com/CINCO.lounge/
Cinco Lounge Map
https://goo.gl/maps/KJPjzg45aP42

Ministerium

Housed in what used to be Lisbon's Ministry of Finance, Ministerium prides itself with special 18th century architecture. The club takes advantage of its historic appleal. Its classic decor however, is a complete opposite to the modern music the DJs play who happens to be the savviest ones in Portugal.

You can't help but dance to the cool techno-electronica soundtrack. If you're in the city on a Saturday, you're in luck. Ministerium as a nightclub only opens on Saturday nights so make sure to check out this hip Lisbon club.
Address: Terreiro do Paço, Lisbon 1100-038
Opening Hours: Sat (11pm-6am)
Ministerium Website
https://www.facebook.com/MinisteriumClub/
Ministerium Map
https://goo.gl/maps/B5tnsdBbuVN2

10

Top 5 Affordable Hotels

<u>ONDE FICAR</u>

Top 5 Affordable Hotels
You don't have to spend loads of cash to avail of comfortable accommodation. You just need to find the top rated but affordable hotels in the city. To help you out, here are the top five hotel

recommendations.

Hotel Borges

Located in Lisbon's most fashionable neighborhood, Chiado, Hotel Borges offers an elegant accommodation at a friendly starting rate of 42.00€ per person per night. The 3-star hotel treats you to a stunning view of Tagus River. It's close to several major attractions including the Museum of Contemporary Art, San Carlos theatres and Chiado Museum.

With close to a hundred rooms available, you can choose from a single to double to triple rooms. Every room gives access to modern amenities. You can even request a room with a balcony for better viewing of the surrounding areas.

Address: Rua Garret N°108 Baixa, Lisbon
Phone: +44 (0) 2071004522
Hotel Borges Website
http://www.hotelborges.com/hotel-overview.html
Hotel Borges Map
https://goo.gl/maps/4zjP29pFZMp

Browns Downtown Hotel

This 3-star has been awarded the Certificate of Excellence winner by TripAdvisor. Browns Downtown Hotel feels like home providing you with all the modern comforts you are used to and more. It is conveniently located near taxi services, train stations and bus stations so guests can get around the city much easier. Plus, it's close to the Tagus River, the Comercio Square and St. George's Castle.

Address: Rua dos Sapateiros, 73 – Lisbon
Phone:+351 213 431 391
Browns Downtown Hotel Website
http://www.brownsdowntown.com/
Browns Downtown Hotel Map

https://goo.gl/maps/6EFUGCvZJB82

Eduardo VII Hotel

This charming 3-star hotel is a wonderful place to stay at with its interesting design reminiscent of the past centuries. While the interior has an old world feel, Eduardo VII hotel does not fall short in providing modern amenities. A big bonus is the hotel is only a few minute walk to the Baixa Chiado area, the Parque Eduardo VII and the Marques de Pombal Square. The room rate starts at 44.02€ per person per night

Address: Av Fontes Pereira de Melo,5 - Lisbon

Eduardo VII Hotel Website

http://www.holeleduardovii.pt/EN/hotel.html?id_referer=ADWORDS&gclid=COnciq_nmckCFVgmvQodj7YNBQ

Eduardo VII Hotel Map

https://goo.gl/maps/EPZpsfR4Ksw

Hotel Roma

Found in one of Lisbon's main avenues, Avenida de Roma, the 3-star Hotel Roma has an ideal location sandwiched between the commercial and residential area. From the hotel, you can easily access the city center. It is also close to the Bairro Alto and Chiado.

The hotel has 263 rooms with single, double, triple and quad rooms available. The rooms are well-equipped with modern facilities and amenities. The best part is the rates are affordable starting from 26.06€ per person per night.

Address: Av. de Roma, 33, Lisbon

Phone: +44 (0) 2071004522

Hotel Roma Website

http://www.hotelroma.pt/

Hotel Roma Map

https://goo.gl/maps/wdnUygUPTFu

Hotel Dom Afonso Henriques

Hotel DAH is ideally situated for tourists to explore magnificent Lisbon. From the hotel, you can reach the city center in less than 10 minutes. It is also close to the airport. Local buses can be easily accessed from this accommodation and so are other means of transport.

The 2-star hotel is small with 39 rooms available but it provides quality accommodation at a great price complete in amenities. The room rates start at 28.00€ per person per night. Request a room with a beautiful view of the city and the stunning Tagus River.

Address: Rua Cristóvão Falcão nº 8, Lisbon
Phone: +44 (0) 2071004522
Hotel Dom Afonso Henriques Website
http://www.hoteldah.com/en
Hotel Dom Afonso Henriques Map
https://goo.gl/maps/6kT9m3JufFL2

11

Top 5 Restaurants

<u>*ONDE COMER*</u>

Top 5 Restaurants

The food in Lisbon is just as exquisite as the sights. There's a mix of luxury and budget restaurants in the city. In this list, you will find places where you can get the most value for your money.

Chicken All Around

If you like chicken then this is a must-try restaurant. This mid-range priced restaurant has a made a name reinventing chicken dishes. As you would guess, the star ingredient in all of the dishes is chicken and the main aim is to expound on chicken dish choices.

Among the menu highlights is the grilled chicken club sandwich served with exciting sauces like the spicy tandoori. It also comes with a Mexican fajita with crunchy salad garnishing. They also serve American barbecue and Jamaican or Thai style chicken. For dessert, order the chunky cheesecake or the crème brûlée de laranja.

Address: Mercado da Ribeira, Lisbon

Phone: +351 21 244 980

Chicken All Around Map

https://goo.gl/maps/fzU6hmk4VNp

IBO Marisqueira

The focus of this restaurant is seafood. IBO Marisqueira serves seafood in all colors, shapes and sizes. Unique with a Mozambican heritage, the restaurant serves traditional recipes which are cooked to perfection. Their seafood platters are not only plated beautifully. They are also served in generous portions.

The menu highlights include the tiger prawns and the variety of shellfish. They have crab, lobster, oyster, mussel and cockle among many others. You will also find meat dishes. To complete your dining experience, try the Laurentina which is the Mozambican national beer.

Address: Rua Cintura do Porto 22 Lisbon

Phone: +351 929 308 068

Opening Hours: Tue-Thu (12:30pm-3:30pm) (7:30pm-11pm) Fri-Sat (12:30pm-3:30pm) (7:30pm-12mn) Sun (12:30pm-3:30pm)

IBO Marisqueira Website

http://www.ibo-restaurante.pt/

IBO Marisqueira Map
https://goo.gl/maps/QzWUfnBwGeR2

Tascardoso

A casual restaurant in Bairro Alto, Tascardoso specializes in serving unpretentious traditional Portuguese cuisine. They have an interesting menu offering a variety of regional dishes. Among their most unique and must-try offering is the corvine which is a croaker fish steak grilled perfectly. Another unusual dish is the cuttlefish that's grilled in its own ink. They call is chocos assados com tinta. Tascardoso has a limited but excellent wine list.

Address: Rua de O Século 242-4, Lisbon 1200-439
Phone: +351 21 342 7578
Tascardoso Website
https://www.facebook.com/pages/Tascardoso/308477135842472
Tascardoso Map
https://goo.gl/maps/mjj9Du9jqqw

O Pitéu da Graça

You will rarely read about this unassuming and homely restaurant in travel guides but it is one of the best kept secrets of Lisbon. As a matter of fact, top chefs in Lisbon come here to eat.

The family-owned restaurant serves traditional Portuguese recipes which were handed down from generation to generation. They serve marinated and spiced Minho-style roast pork as well as turbot fillet served with pepper rice and tomato. Their plates are colorful and the dishes are absolutely flavorful. You can get here through the tram no. 28.

Address: Largo da Graça 95, Lisbon 1170-165
Phone: +351 21 887 1067
Opening Hours: Mon-Fri (12nn-3pm) (7pm-10:30pm) Sat (12nn-3pm)
O Pitéu da Graça Map

https://goo.gl/maps/aqKD2L3kexn

Feitoria Restaurante & Wine Bar
Aside from Chef Joao Rodrigues' Michelin-star menu, this Lisbon restaurant in Belem is sought after because of its great venue. Set by the waterfront, Feitoria Restaurante & Wine Bar provides diners with a compelling view of the Targus River.

The chef serves inventive traditional Spanish, Southern European and Portuguse dishes plated beautifully. The superb dining experience starts off with a hot or cold starter. For the entree, you would want to try the sautéed Algarve scarlet shrimp with fresh cucumber garnishing. And for the main course, the smoked salami is exemplary. The succulent grouper with green peas is like no other. Another highlight from the world class menu is the tender veal loin served with wild mushrooms. The restaurant also has an excellent and extensive wine list. Do try something you haven't tasted from home.

Dining at Feitoria Restaurante & Wine Bar is a little more expensive than others in this list. However, it is worth the try. Expect nothing less than an exciting gastronomic adventure from chef Joao Rodrigues and his team. You would want to book a seat in advance. If you're looking for a unique dining experience, order the creative menu but do so at least 2 days in advance.
Address: Altis Belém Hotel & Spa, Lisbon, 1400-038
Phone: +351 21 040 0200
Opening Hours: Mon-Sat (7:30pm-11pm)
Feitoria Restaurante & Wine Bar Website
http://www.restaurantefeitoria.com/en/
Feitoria Restaurante & Wine Bar Map
https://goo.gl/maps/cVyBMUUg78J2

12

Special Things You Can ONLY DO in Lisbon

EXPERIÊNCIAS ÚNICAS EM LISBOA
Special Things You Can ONLY DO in Lisbon

What make a city special are the unique things you can experience from it. Do try these things while you're in the charming capital of Portugal.

Check out Campo Pequeno

Located in Uptown Lisbon, Campo Pequeno is a monumental building according to Moorish style. Constructed in 1892, the building features cupolas atop the main towers with a bullring that can accommodate 9,000 spectators.

Today, the bullring is used for bullfighting on Thursdays in season. It is also occasionally used for circus, concerts and other shows. Within Campo Pequeno, you will find cinemas, restaurants and a shopping mall too. To get here, take the Metro going to Campo Pequeno Station.

Campo Pequeno Bullring Map
https://goo.gl/maps/UFMk4PiJwLC2

Take the Antediluvian Eléctrico No. 28 to See the Historical Areas of Lisbon.

There used to be horse-drawn trams but in 1903 they were replaced by the eléctricos. This ride will take you to an interesting trip through the historical sites of Lisbon.

Stop by at Casa dos Bicos

Dubbed as a 16th century architectural curiosity, Casa dos Bicos means "house of spikes." A total of 1125 diamond-shaped stones adorn its face. Many structures were destroyed by the earthquake but this palace stood strong. The arched windows are true to Portuguese Manueline style. It is only open during temporary exhibitions but even the view from the outside is spectacular.

Casa dos Bicos Map
https://goo.gl/maps/inPALJqa9MA2

Sightseeing at Miradouro das Portas do Sol and Miradouro de Santa Luzia

These locations stand over the medieval and history-rich area of

Lisbon. From here, you can gaze at the immense beauty of the city. Miradouro de Santa Luzia introduces you to Alfama. It greets visitors with a marvelous view overlooking the river, the beautiful churches and the medieval houses. At Miradouro das Portas do Sol, you will find St Vincent's statue with a boat in one arm and two ravens on the other. He is Lisbon's patron saint holding the city's symbols.

Miradouro das Portas do Sol Map
https://goo.gl/maps/cnsCPkdZEJ62
Miradouro de Santa Luzia Map
https://goo.gl/maps/jJdy7e2cw6T2

Visit a 16th-century monument, the Sao Vicente de Fora Church.
Built in 1582 in honor of the crusaders and Portuguese soldiers who fought the Moors, the church was ruined during the earthquake but was restored in 1855. You can enter the church from the gate to the right. Admire the 18th century tiled panels that adorn its interior. The tiles depict some of the scenes from LaFontaine's Fables. You can also climb up to the roof and get a marvelous view of the Tagus River, the National Pantheon and the whole of Alfama.

Sao Vicente de Fora Church Map
https://goo.gl/maps/WVBkkyLAeWH2

Explore Saint George's Castle.
This massive and millennium old structure is visible from nearly everywhere in Lisbon. Some sections that were built way back in the 6th century still stand. They were fortified by rulers from the Romans to the Visigoths to the Moors. It served as the residence of Moorish royals. When King Alfonso Henriques and the crusaders captured the walls, the castle was dedicated and named after England's patron saint, St. George.

Today, this historic castle is an oasis of peace and tranquility offering a picturesque view of the city. At the main gate, visitors are welcomed by the first king's statue along with cannons which is a constant reminder of the castle's initial purpose. You can climb up the towers for the views, stop by at the archeological museums in the underground chambers or relax in the beautiful gardens.

Explore the castle from March to October between 9am and 9pm, from November to February between 9am and 6pm.
Saint George's Castle Website
http://castelodesaojorge.pt/en
Saint George's Castle Map
https://goo.gl/maps/HzXDvfViKn62

Watch the sunset from Doca do Jardim do Tabaco.
This is one of Alfama's prided attractions. Its name means "Tobacco Garden Dock" as it used to be the city's main depot for tobacco. Jardim do Tabaco offers a stunning view of the sunset at the breathtaking Tagus River. Known as the trendiest waterfront, it has plenty of excellent restaurants with outdoor seating. There are trendy shops and nightclubs here too.
Doca do Jardim do Tabaco Map
https://goo.gl/maps/Ujk83sWDarR2

Stop by at Fronteira Palace
Constructed in 1640, this beautiful residence located in the suburb of Benfica in Uptown Lisbon has stunning gardens, spectacular decorative tile work, oil paintings and frescoed panels. Tourists come here to walk along the formal gardens with tiles that depict religious scenes, battles and hunting. There are magnificent fountains, statues and busts of Portuguese kings too.

To book the guided tour in advance, you may call (+351) 21 778 2023.

It is a private residence but you can join a guided tour to this lovely palace through the rooms and gardens. The guided tour occurs every 30 minutes from 10:30 to 12nn on Mondays to Saturdays.

Fronteira Palace Map
https://goo.gl/maps/oAYfVwQ7UwA2

13

3-Day Itinerary

A 3-Day Itinerary

Day One

6:30am Breakfast at the Hotel
7:00am Take the antediluvian eléctrico no. 28 to Alfama
7:30am Enjoy the view at Miradouro de Santa Luzia and Explore Miradouro das Portas Do Sol
8:30am Walk to Sao Vicente de Fora Church for a quick peek
9:00am Visit Saint George's Castle
10:30am Explore the sights around the Comercio Square including the Casa dos Bicos
Check out the tourist shops in the area as well
12:00pm Taste the traditional grilled fish dishes from restaurants nearby
1:30pm Visit the Decorative Arts Museum
3:30pm Visit Museu Nacional do Azulejo
6:00pm Watch the sunset from a café at Doca do Jardim do Tabaco
7:30pm Check out the trendy shops
9:30pm Dinner by the waterfront
11:00pm Check out Station nightclub

Day Two

6:30am Breakfast at the Hotel
9:00am Check out one of the museums in Belém
11:00am Take a taxi to Fronteira Palace, Uptown for a guided tour

1:00pm Lunch
2:30pm Head to Calouste Gulbenkian Museum
4:30pm Visit Campo Pequeno
5:30pm Stop by at Amoreiras or Colombo, one of the largest shopping malls in Europe
7:00pm Have a quick bite at Cafe Versailles
9:00pm Dinner

Day Three
6:30am Breakfast at the Hotel
8:00am Wander around Praça do Comércio
9:00am Check out the stores at Rua Augusta
11:00am Walk along Rossio
12:00nn Lunch at Café Nicola
1:30pm Praça dos Restauradores
2:30pm Estação do Rossio
3:00pm Visit Rua Áurea and Rua da Prata for the finest gold and silver
4:30pm Elevador de Santa Justa
5:30pm Stop for snacks
9:00pm Dinner at a restuarant of your choice
10:00pm Stop by at Clube da Esquina

14

Conclusion

I want to thank you for reading this book! I sincerely hope that you received value from it!

If you received value from this book, I want to ask you for a favour. Would you be kind enough to leave a review for this book on Amazon?

Ó Copyright 2016 by Gary Jones – All rights reserved.
This document is geared towards providing exact and reliable information in regards to the topic and issue covered. The publication is sold with the idea that the publisher is not required to render accounting, officially permitted, or otherwise, qualified services. If advice is necessary, legal or professional, a practiced individual in the profession should be ordered.
- From a Declaration of Principles which was accepted and approved equally by a Committee of the American Bar Association and a Committee of Publishers and Associations.
In no way is it legal to reproduce, duplicate, or transmit any part of this document in either electronic means or in printed format. Recording of this publication is strictly prohibited and any storage of this document is not allowed unless with written permission from the publisher. All rights reserved.

The information provided herein is stated to be truthful and consistent, in that any liability, in terms of inattention or otherwise, by any usage or abuse of any policies, processes, or directions contained within is the solitary and utter responsibility of the recipient reader. Under no circumstances will any legal responsibility or blame be held against the publisher for any reparation, damages, or monetary loss due to the information herein, either directly or indirectly.

Respective authors own all copyrights not held by the publisher.

The information herein is offered for informational purposes solely, and is universal as so. The presentation of the information is without contract or any type of guarantee assurance.

The trademarks that are used are without any consent, and the publication of the trademark is without permission or backing by the trademark owner. All trademarks and brands within this book are for clarifying purposes only and are the owned by the owners themselves, not affiliated with this document.